Let's Explore

How many are there?

by Henry Pluckrose

W
FRANKLIN WATTS
NEW YORK • LONDON • SYDNEY

Author's note

This book is one of a series which has been designed to encourage young readers to think about the everyday concepts that form part of their world. The text and photographs complement each other, and both elements combine to provide starting points for discussion. Although each book is complete in itself, each title links closely with others in the set, so presenting an ideal platform for learning.

I have consciously avoided 'writing down' to my readers. Young children like to know the 'real' words for things, and are better able to express themselves when they can use correct terms with confidence.

Young children learn from the experiences they share with adults around them. The child offers his or her ideas which are then developed and extended through the adult. The books in this series are a means for the child and adult to share informal talk, photographs and text, and the ideas which accompany them.

One particular element merits comment. Information books are also reading books. Like a successful story book, an effective information book will be turned to again and again. As children develop, their appreciation of the significance of fact develops too. The young child who asks 'What is a number?' may subsequently and more provocatively ask, 'What is the biggest number in the world?' Thoughts take time to generate. Hopefully books like those in this series provide the momentum for this.

Henry Pluckrose

Contents

One, two, three, four, five...
Everywhere you look,
you can see numbers.
On the door of your house,
on the front of the bus,
on your telephone.
Where else can you
see numbers?

5

Each number has a different shape.
Numbers can be written
in figures and in words.

Can you match these words
to the figures opposite?

one two three four

five six seven

eight nine ten

7

There are lots of sheep
on the hillside.

We use numbers to count the sheep.
How many sheep can you count?

When you were small,
you probably used your hands
to help you to count to ten.

11

How many oranges are there?

Danielle adds two more oranges.
How many oranges
are there now?

How many children are at the party?
Two of the children go home.

Take away two children.
How many children are left?

How many pieces of cake
can you count?
Divide the cake
between the children.
How many pieces
will each child have?

How many trucks are there?

Do you know how many wheels
are on each truck?

Two sets of four wheels
equals eight wheels in all.

20

Sometimes we count in groups.
We have special words
for groups of numbers.
A 'pair' is a group of two.
What kinds of things
come in pairs?

How many shoes are there?
How many pairs can you make?

We call six an 'even' number.
It can be divided into pairs.

How many socks
are hanging
on this washing line?

How many pairs can you make?

Seven is an 'odd' number.
When we put the socks into pairs,
there is one sock left over.

The children are running a race.

Jack is the winner, he came first.

Ben came second.

Josh came third.

Who will stand on block one?
Who will stand on blocks
two and three?

We can use numbers to measure.

We can measure weight.

We can measure size.

We can measure distance.

How many kilometres
away is Paris?

It is easier to count small numbers,
but sometimes we need
to count large numbers too.
You could even count
all the people in this crowd!

100 – one hundred

1,000 – one thousand

1,000,000 – one million

Index

First published in 1999 by
Franklin Watts
96 Leonard Street
London
EC2A 4XD

Franklin Watts Australia
14 Mars Road
Lane Cove
NSW 2066

Copyright © Franklin Watts 1999

ISBN 0 7496 3572 X

Dewey Decimal
Classification Number 513

A CIP catalogue record for this book is
available from the British Library

Series editor: Louise John
Series designer: Jason Anscomb
Series consultant: Peter Patilla

Printed in Hong Kong

Picture Credits:
Steve Shott Photography pp. cover and title
page, 6, 11, 12, 13, 14, 15, 16, 19, 20, 22, 23, 24,
25, 27; Bubbles pp. 26 (Jennie Woodcock);
The Stock Market p. 29; AA Photo Library
p. 28; Bruce Coleman p. 8/9 (Jorg & Petra
Wegner); Robert Harding p. 31; Image Bank
p. 4 (Grant Faint).
With thanks to our models:
Reid Burns, Karim Chehab, Alex Dymock,
Melissa Eedle, Danielle Grimmett-Gardiner,
Charlie Newton, Robert Orbeney,
Alice Snedden.